A TRIBUTE TO

Dad

A heartwarming collection

of stories, quotes

and writings

just for fathers

ISBN 1-889116-13-0

Printed in the United States of America

First U.S. Edition
Second Printing

Cover design & Interior format and typeset by:
Paragon Communications Group, Inc., Tulsa, Oklahoma

Published by
PENBROOKE PUBLISHING
Tulsa, Oklahoma

A TRIBUTE TO

Dad

PENBROOKE
PUBLISHING

TULSA, OKLAHOMA

Dedicated To:

No man can possibly know what life means, what the world means, what anything means, until he has a child and loves it. And then the whole universe changes and nothing will ever again seem exactly as it seemed before.

Lafcadio Hearn

Dads are stone skimmers, mud wallowers, water wallopers, ceiling swoopers, shoulder gallopers, upsy-downsy, over-and-through, round-and-about whooshers. Dads are smugglers and secret sharers.

Helen Thomson

8

Success is measured in many ways; not the least of which is the way a child describes their father when talking to a friend.

Anonymous

When one becomes a father, then first one becomes a son. Standing by the crib of one's own baby, with that world-old pang of compassion and protectiveness toward this so little creature that has all its course to run, the heart flies back in yearning and gratitude to those who felt just so towards one's self. Then for the first time one understands the homely succession of sacrifices and pains by which life is transmitted down the stumbling generations of men.

Christopher Morley

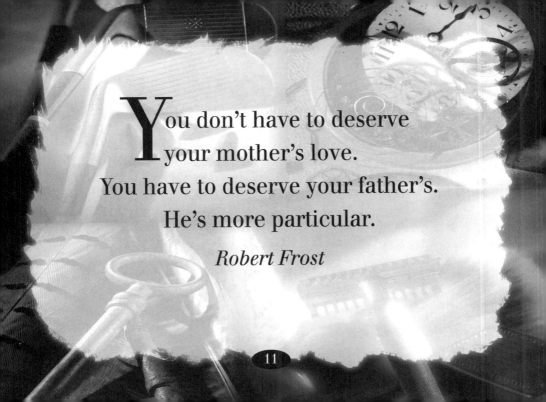

You don't have to deserve
your mother's love.
You have to deserve your father's.
He's more particular.

Robert Frost

When I was a boy of fourteen, my father was so ignorant I could hardly stand to have the old man around. But when I got to be twenty-one, I was astounded at how much the old man had learned in seven years.

Mark Twain

G overn a family as you would cook a small fish—very gently.

Anonymous

A father is a banker provided by nature.

French Proverb

When a father is indulgent, he is more indulgent than a mother. Little ones treat their mother as the authority of rule, and their fathers as the authority of dispensation.

Frederick W. Faber

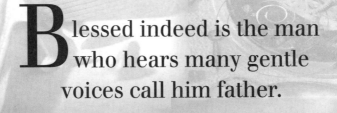

B lessed indeed is the man who hears many gentle voices call him father.

Lydia Child

Children are poor men's riches.

Thomas Fuller

My earliest recollections are of being dressed up and allowed to come down to dance for a group of gentlemen who applauded and laughed as I pirouetted before them. Finally, my father would pick me up and hold me high in the air. He dominated my life as long as he lived, and was the love of my life for many years after he died.

Eleanor Roosevelt

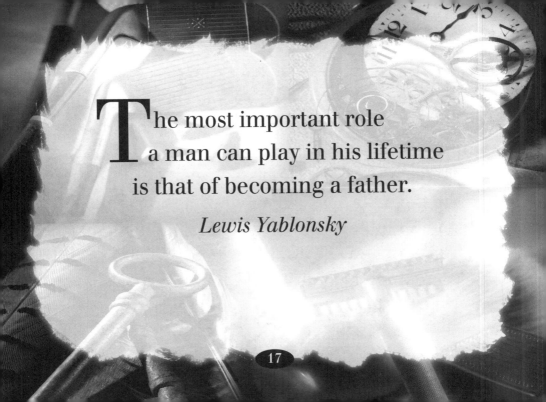

The most important role
a man can play in his lifetime
is that of becoming a father.

Lewis Yablonsky

I realized that more than any other person, my father taught me many of life's most important lessons. I was taught them with love and patience and compassion, and I know they are the basis for much of who and what I am today. So subtle were his teachings, though, that I never knew they were his until I became a parent myself and saw my father in me as I began to shape my own children's lives.

Today. . .I strive to be as careful and gentle with my son as my father was with his. I am trying very hard to be these things because I understand that what I say and do will live with him long beyond my time, just as what my father said and did survived his time. And though I know we are different, I am grateful for what I have of my father in me. It is my gift, my promise to myself and my children.

Kenneth Barrett, "Promises"

A man's children and his garden both reflect the amount of weeding done during the growing season.

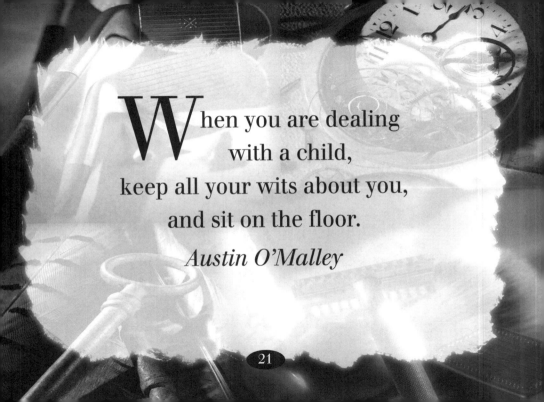

When you are dealing
with a child,
keep all your wits about you,
and sit on the floor.

Austin O'Malley

BEING A FATHER

But after you've raised them
and educated and gowned them,
They just take their little fingers
and wrap you around them.
Being a father
Is quite a bother
But I like it, rather.

Ogden Nash

There are three ways to get something done: do it yourself, hire someone, or forbid your kids to do it.

Monta Crane

I've wondered, over the years, as I've recalled these moments with my father, what they're supposed to teach me about life. I can't say there's any lesson, except the sheer pleasure of his company, which was a great gift, and which I gather is sometimes hard to come by between fathers and sons.

Scott Simon

Life's journey is circular, it appears.
The years don't carry us away
from our fathers—
they return us to them.

Michel Marriott

If you ever become a father, I think the strangest and strongest sensation of your life will be hearing for the first time the thin cry of your own child. For a moment you have the strange feeling of being double; but there is something more, quite impossible to analyze— perhaps the echo in a man's heart of all the sensations felt by all fathers and mothers at a similar instant in the past.

It is a tender, but also a very ghostly feeling.

Lafcadio Hearn

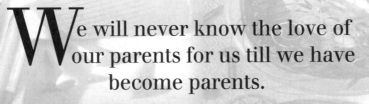

Wwe will never know the love of our parents for us till we have become parents.

Henry Ward Beecher

Fatherhood is pretending the present you love most is soap-on-a-rope.

Bill Cosby

She climbed into my lap and curled into the crook of my left arm. I couldn't move that arm, but I could cradle Ashtin in it. I could kiss the top of her head. And I could have no doubt that this was one of the sweetest moments in my life.

Dennis Byrd, about his daughter

I f you live without being a father you will die without being a human being.

Russian Proverb

Parenthood isn't a picnic.
Dad may work from sun to sun,
but as a father he's never done.

William Wilkins

At my father's table he liked to have, as often as he could, some sensible friend or neighbor to converse with, and always took care to start some ingenious or useful topic for discourse, which might tend to improve the minds of his children. By this means he turned our attention to what was good, just, and prudent in the conduct of life; and little or no notice was ever taken of what related to the victuals on the table, whether it was well or ill dressed, in or out of season, of good or bad flavor, preferable or inferior to this or that other thing of the kind, so that I was brought up in such a perfect inattention to these matters as to be quite indifferent to what kind of food was set before me, and so unobservant of it that to this day if I am asked I can scarcely tell a few hours after dinner what I dined upon.

Benjamin Franklin

His heritage to his children wasn't words or possessions, but an unspoken treasure, the treasure of his example as a man and a father. More than anything I have, I'm trying to pass that on to my children.

Will Rogers

Happy is he that is happy in his children.
Thomas Fuller

All men know their children
mean more than life.
Euripides

Nothing in literature prepares a father for his role. Motherhood is swamped with books—poetic, fictional, factual. No authority discourses on the prenatal and postpartum care of young fathers.

Frederic F. Van de Water

A father's words are like a thermostat that sets the temperature in the house.

Paul Lewis

One father is worth more than a hundred schoolmasters.

George Herbert

It is a waste of breath for the father to order his sons to keep their temper, to behave like gentlemen, or to be good sportsmen, if he does or is himself none of these things.

Emily Post

36

My father's influence on me is undeniable, but it is manifest principally in the details of my everyday life.

Jean Renoir

COME HOME, FATHER

Father, dear Father, come home with me now,
The clock in the belfry strikes one;
You said you were coming right home from the shop
As soon as your day's work was done.

Henry Clay Work

I can remember playing under the big wooden desk in [my father's] office. My mother didn't like us to chew gum, so we'd go into his office and he'd feed us gum under the desk.

John F. Kennedy, Jr.

A child enters your home and for the next twenty years makes so much noise you can hardly stand it. The child departs, leaving the house so silent you think you are going mad.

John Andrew Holmes

As a child I read hoping to learn everything, so I could be like my father.

Annie Dillard

Papa never climbed Everest or made the *Guinness Book of World Records*. He never read the classics or saw an original painting by Braque. He never played baseball and rarely won at bocce ball. He was born poor and, in spite of his working hard all his life, he was always poor. He was proud, self-taught, and left no debts. If he had any hidden dreams, other than of being a good man, a committed father, and a loving husband, no one ever knew about them. If deep regrets, fears, or personal doubts tormented him, he never stated them. I am aware that years of having known and loved my father have transformed him from Papa, the simple human being, into Papa, the near saint. And I've come to the conclusion that there is nothing wrong with that.

Leo Buscaglia, Papa, My Father

My father was honorable—he always knew exactly what that word meant. He had integrity. His "One does not do that sort of thing," his "No it is *not* right," sounded throughout my childhood and were final for all of us.

Doris Lessing, "My Father"

Yet in my lineaments
they trace some features
of my father's face.

George Gordon, Lord Byron

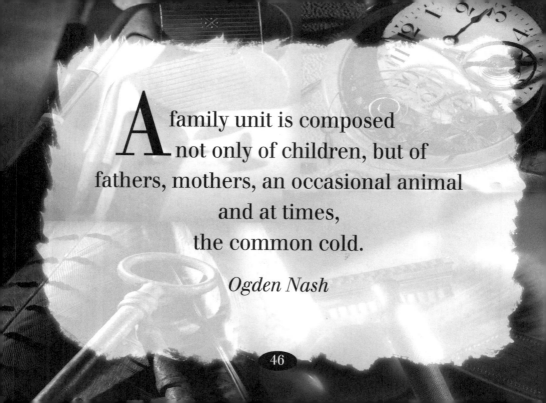

A family unit is composed not only of children, but of fathers, mothers, an occasional animal and at times, the common cold.

Ogden Nash

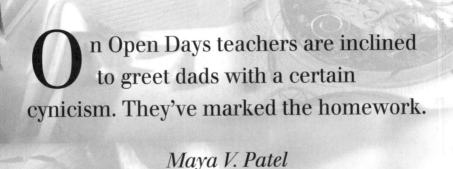

On Open Days teachers are inclined to greet dads with a certain cynicism. They've marked the homework.

Maya V. Patel

To show a child what
has once delighted you,
to find the child's delight added to your
own so that there is now a double delight
seen in the glow of trust and affection,
this is happiness.

J. B. Priestly

Papa was easygoing and of a happy disposition, and like his father gave one the feeling that the world was on the whole, a happy place.

Marguerite de Angeli

My father was not an extraordinary man as to where he arrived, but he was extraordinary in the distance he advanced. Although he died more than twenty-five years ago, not a day passes without my thinking of him.

Edward A. Filene

Children are unpredictable.
You never know what
inconsistency they're going
to catch you in next.

Franklin P. Jones

My dear father is a very peculiar person. He is naturally stern, and has exaggerated notions of authority, but these things go with high and noble qualities. . .I admire such qualities as he has—fortitude, integrity. I loved him for his courage in adverse circumstances which were yet felt by him more literally than I could feel them. I have loved him so and love him.

Elizabeth Barrett Browning

I n my struggle to be a writer, it was [my father] who supported and backed me and explained me.

John Steinbeck

It was the dexterity with his fingers that delighted his children before they could potter along the lanes at his heels or read his books. He would twist a sheet of paper beneath a pair of scissors and out would drop an elephant, a stag, or a monkey, with trunks, horns, and tails delicately and exactly formed. Or, taking a pencil, he would draw beast after beast— an art he practiced almost unconsciously as he read, so that the flyleaves of his books swarm with owls and donkeys.

Virginia Woolf

MY FATHER

My father's face is brown with sun,
His body is tall and limber.
His hands are gentle with beast or child
And strong as hardwood timber.

Frances Frost

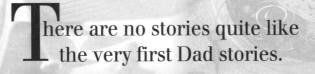

There are no stories quite like
the very first Dad stories.

H. Dalton

A father is someone who carries pictures
where his money used to be.

Anonymous

My father was two men, one sympathetic and intuitional, the other critical and logical; altogether they formed a combination that could not be thrown off its feet.

Julian Hawthorne

Performance under stress is one test of effective leadership. It may also be the proof of accomplishment when it comes to evaluating the quality of a father.

Gordon MacDonald

If there is any one thing which I most like to recall in connection with my father, it is that he grew throughout his life. From him I derived a momentum of the spirit which has carried me to this day, and which I trust may speed me ever to new goals.

John Holmes

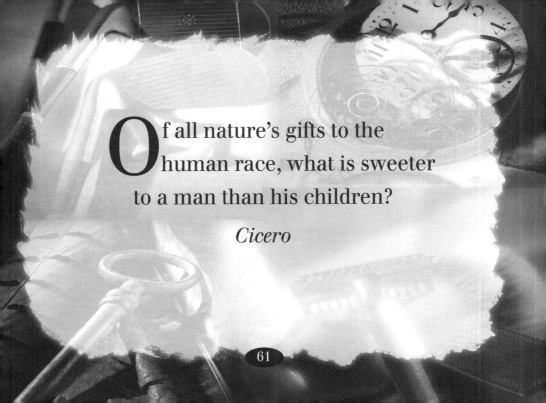

Of all nature's gifts to the human race, what is sweeter to a man than his children?

Cicero

Much of my childhood's happiness was owing to my father. He could spin fairy tales as enthralling as *Alice in Wonderland*, making them up as he went along, with an unfailing flow of fancy. Some of them were serials, and ran for months. Every night there was a fresh attack or a fresh stratagem—each a new delight to the little girl into whose eager ears the tale was poured.

Alice Stone Blackwell,
about her father, Henry B. Blackwell

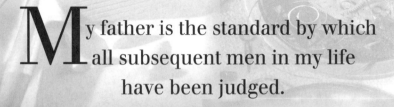

My father is the standard by which
all subsequent men in my life
have been judged.

Kathryn McCarthy Graham

In 1880 when I was a child, I asked my father for a cent. He heard me gravely and then informed me just as gravely that it looked to him as if a Democratic President would be elected that fall, and it behooved every prudent man to exercise especial thrift. Therefore, he would be obliged to deny my request.

Calvin Coolidge

A dad is a man haunted by death, fears, anxieties. But who seems to his children a haven from all harm. And who makes them certain that whatever happens, it will all come right.

Clara Ortega

I cannot remember having ever heard a single sentence uttered by my mother in the nature of moral or religious instruction. My father made an effort or two. When he caught me imitating him by pretending to smoke a toy pipe, he advised me very earnestly never to follow his example in any way; and his sincerity so impressed me that to this day I have never smoked. . . . He taught me to regard him as an unsuccessful man with many undesirable habits, as a warning and not as a model. In fact, he did himself some injustice lest I should grow up like him; and I now see that this anxiety on his part was admirable and lovable; and that he was really just what he so carefully strove not to be: that is, a model father.

George Bernard Shaw

Across his front was a gold watch
chain with a big tick-tock watch
on the end.
All about him was safe.

Naomi Mitchison

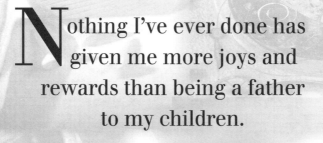

Nothing I've ever done has given me more joys and rewards than being a father to my children.

Bill Cosby

We think of a father as an old, or at least a middle-aged man. The astounding truth is that most fathers are young men, and that they make their greatest sacrifices in their youth. I never meet a young man in a public park on Sunday morning wheeling his first baby in a perambulator without feeling an ache of reverence.

James Douglas

It is no new observation, I believe, that a lover in most cases has no rival so much to be feared as the father.

Charles Lamb

THE LITTLE BOY LOST

Father, father, where are you going?
O do not walk so fast.
Speak, father, speak to your little boy
Or else I shall be lost.

William Blake

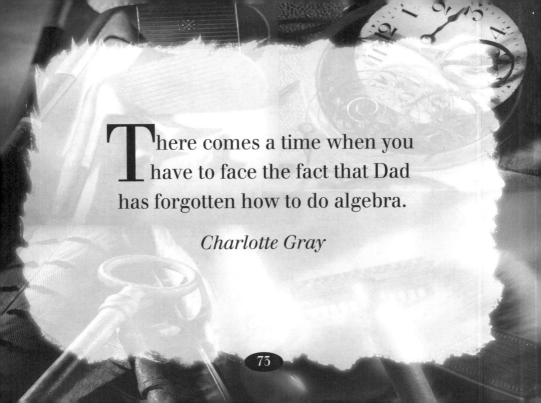

There comes a time when you have to face the fact that Dad has forgotten how to do algebra.

Charlotte Gray

73

The words that a father speaks to his children in the privacy of home are not heard by the world, but, as in whispering-galleries, they are clearly heard at the end and by posterity.

Jean Paul Richter

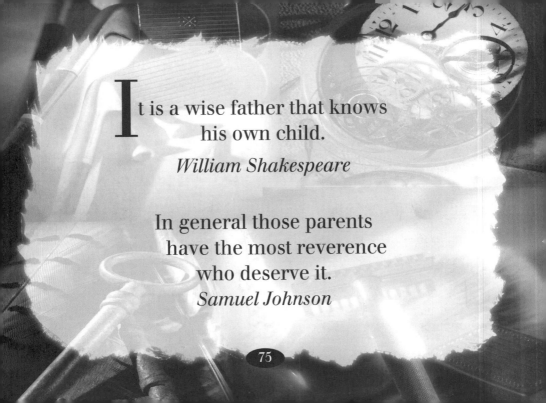

It is a wise father that knows
his own child.
William Shakespeare

In general those parents
have the most reverence
who deserve it.
Samuel Johnson

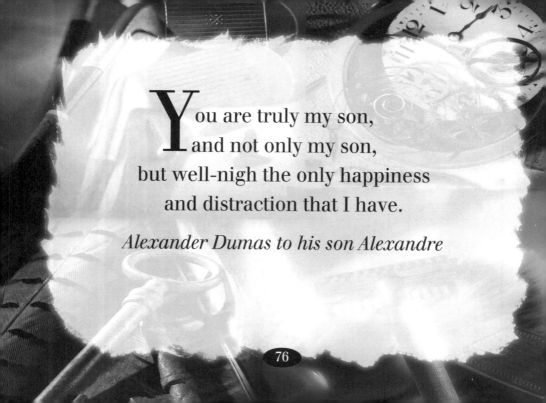

You are truly my son,
and not only my son,
but well-nigh the only happiness
and distraction that I have.

Alexander Dumas to his son Alexandre

The child you want to raise as an upright and honorable person requires a lot more of your time than your money.

George Varky

FATHERLY ADVICE

Look thou character. Give thy thoughts no tongue,
Nor any unproportioned thought his act.
Be thou familiar, but by no means vulgar.
Those friends thou hast, and their adoption tried,
Grapple them unto thy soul with hoops of steel.
But do not dull thy palm with entertainment
Of each new-hatched, unfledged courage.
Beware of entrance to a quarrel. But, being in,
Bear't that th' opposed may beware of thee.
Give every man thine ear, but few thy voice.

Take each man's censure, but reserve thy judge-
ment. Costly thy habit as thy purse can buy,
But not expressed in fancy; rich, not gaudy;
For the apparel oft proclaims the man. . . .
Neither a borrower nor a lender be,
For loan oft loses both itself and friend,
And borrowing dulleth edge of husbandry.
This above all: to thine own self be true,
And it must follow, as the night the day,
Though canst not then be false to any man.

William Shakespeare
Polonius to his son, Laertes

We never know the love of our parents till we become parents ourselves. When we first bend over the cradle of our own child, God throws back the temple door, and reveals to us the sacredness and mystery of the father's and mother's love to ourselves.

Henry Ward Beecher

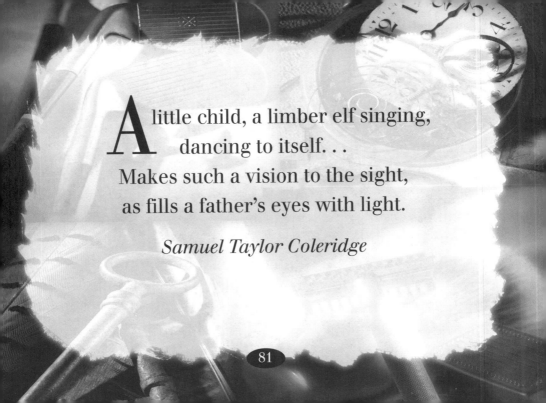

A little child, a limber elf singing,
    dancing to itself. . .
Makes such a vision to the sight,
as fills a father's eyes with light.

Samuel Taylor Coleridge

No one knows the true worth of a man but his family. The dreary man drowsing, drop-jawed, in the commuter train, the office bore, the taciturn associate—may be the pivot of a family's life, welcomed with hugs, told the day's news, asked for advice. No longer Mr. B., but Dad. No longer a nonentity but a man possessed of skills and wisdom; courageous and capable, patient and kind. Respected and loved.

Pam Brown

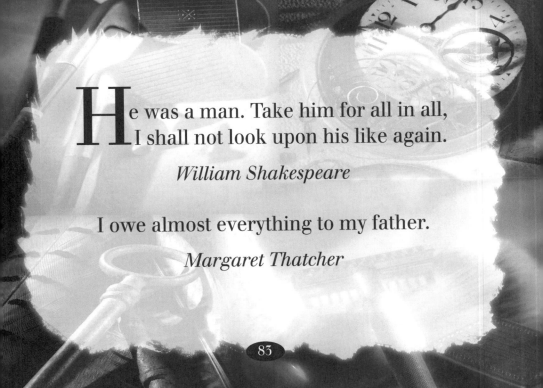

He was a man. Take him for all in all,
I shall not look upon his like again.

William Shakespeare

I owe almost everything to my father.

Margaret Thatcher

83

Even the best of good fathers,
in spite of loving their children,
are quite humanly often inconvenienced
and annoyed by them.

Spurgeon English

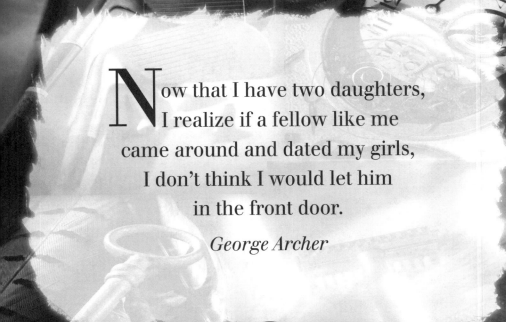

Now that I have two daughters,
I realize if a fellow like me
came around and dated my girls,
I don't think I would let him
in the front door.

George Archer

85

ONLY A DAD

Only a dad but he gives his all,
To smooth the way for his children small,
Doing with courage stern and grim
The deeds that his father did for him.
This is the line that for him I pen:
Only a dad, but the best of men.

Edgar Guest

The chances are that you will never be elected president of the country, write the great American novel, make a million dollars, stop pollution, end racial conflict, or save the world. However valid it may be to work at any of these goals, there is another one of higher priority— to be an effective parent.

Landrum R. Bolling

Grandfathers should always live long enough to dramatize their old age for their grandchildren in lovable and understandable form. Children so favored receive an impression that does not desert them soon.

Frances Lester Warner

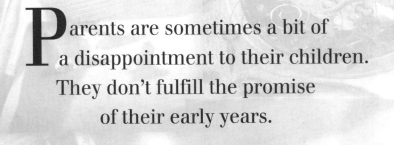

Parents are sometimes a bit of a disappointment to their children. They don't fulfill the promise of their early years.

Anthony Powell

Father usually made an appearance about tea-time which was heralded by a great deal of banging and foot-scraping outside before his actual arrival indoors. Having deposited in the corner of the scullery by the copper his perks for the day, a mess of greens, a sack of tail-corn for the chickens or a brace of rabbits—for he seldom returned home empty-handed—he would stand for

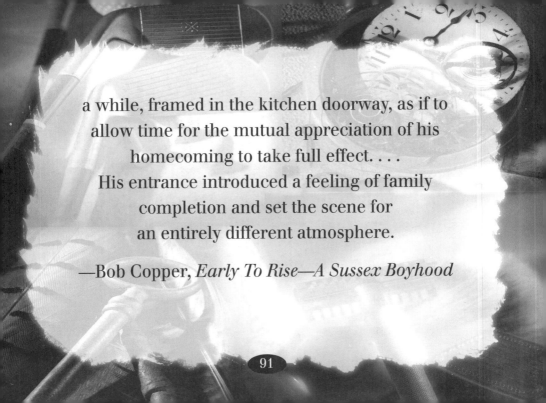

a while, framed in the kitchen doorway, as if to allow time for the mutual appreciation of his homecoming to take full effect. . . .
His entrance introduced a feeling of family completion and set the scene for an entirely different atmosphere.

—Bob Copper, *Early To Rise—A Sussex Boyhood*

In every dispute between parent and child, both cannot be right, but they may be, and usually are, both wrong. It is this situation which gives family life its peculiar hysterical charm.

Isaac Rosenfeld

Of the many things that I owe to
my father, the one for which I am
most grateful is the example
of a great and beautiful life.

Alice Stone Blackwell,
about her father, Henry B. Blackwell

I treasured the nature walks Father and I took together. Father could hide in the bushes and whistle bird call so convincingly that the birds he imitated came to him. He taught me the names of the stars, and how to distinguish the harmless snakes and pick them up without fear.

Margaret Bourke White

Be kind to thy father, for when thou were young,
Who loved thee as fondly as he?
He caught the first accents that fell from thy tongue,
And joined in thy innocent glee.

Margaret Courtney

We do not care how many wrinkles he may have or how his rheumatism makes him limp or how the gray colors his hair, he is still the same great man and the object of our love and adoration.

Leroy Brownlow

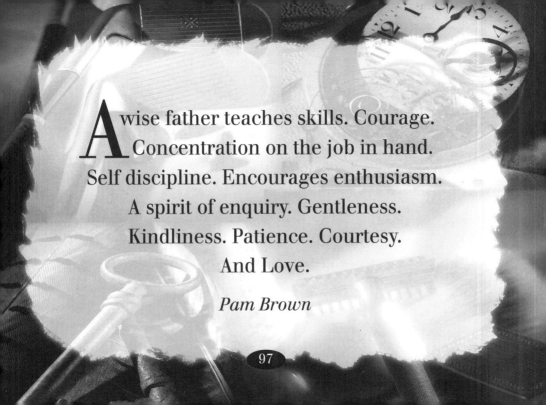

A wise father teaches skills. Courage. Concentration on the job in hand. Self discipline. Encourages enthusiasm. A spirit of enquiry. Gentleness. Kindliness. Patience. Courtesy. And Love.

Pam Brown

I remember being at a point below [my father's] knees and looking up at the vast length of him. He was six foot three; his voice was big. He was devastatingly attractive—even to his daughter as a child. His voice was so beautiful, so enveloping. He was just bigger and better than anyone else.

Anjelica Huston

Fathers should be neither seen nor heard. That is the only proper basis for family life!

Oscar Wilde, An Ideal Husband

Fathers are something else.
They always give up their turn
by saying something like,
"Go ask your mother.
She knows about things like that."

Mary Kuczkir

There are times when parenthood
seems nothing but feeding
the mouth that bites you.

Peter De Vries

101

My father early gave me to understand that a sound and serviceable body was essential for a happy and productive life. For ten years of my boyhood we spent the summers camping out in tents, usually on a lovely and uninhabited island on the coast of Maine. There one learned to row, swim and sail, to chop, saw and lug wood, to fish and forage and to do the camp chores. There was, too, a comfortable sloop yacht in which we cruised the New England coast. My father taught us, not by precept, but by example or letting us learn by doing; so that we could turn our hands to pretty much anything connected with the independent, self-reliant life of the New England seacoast in those contentful days.

Samuel A. Eliot

No man can tell but he that loves his children, how many delicious accents make a man's heart dance in the pretty conversation of those dear pledges: their childishness, their stammering, their little angers, their innocence, their imperfections, their necessities are so many little emanations of joy and comfort to him that delights in their persons and society.

Jeremy Taylor, Twenty-Five Sermons

By looking at us, listening to us,
hearing us, respecting our opinions,
affirming our value, giving us a sense of dignity,
he was unquestionably
our most influential teacher.

Leo Buscaglia, Papa, My Father

LETTER TO DAD

This letter comes to thank you, Dad,
For needed words of praise;
The counsel and the guidance, too,
That shaped my grown-up days.
No words of mine can tell you, Dad,
The things I really feel;
But you must know my love for you
Is lasting, warm and real.

Reginald Holmes

Dads don't need to be tall
and broadshouldered and
handsome and clever.
Love makes them so.

Pam Brown

The father who holds the baby
only when it is sweet and fresh;
who plays on the nursery floor
when things go along like a song;
who gingerly tiptoes away at times of tears
or disciplinary show-downs,
is just a dilettante papa,
with a touch of the coward,
and not a complete father.

Samuel S. Drury

I do not think my life could possibly have changed more than it did by becoming a father. And when my son looks up at me and breaks into his wonderful toothless smile, my eyes fill up and I know that having him is the best thing I will ever do.

Dan Greenberg

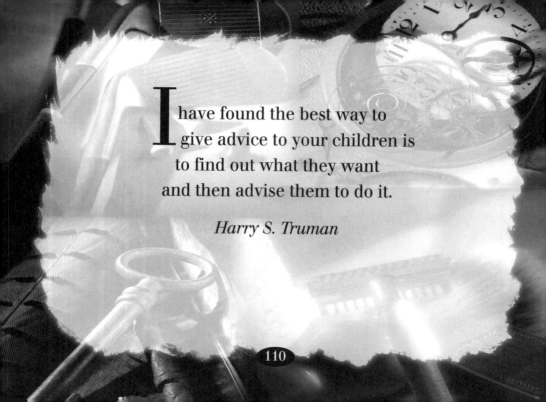

I have found the best way to give advice to your children is to find out what they want and then advise them to do it.

Harry S. Truman

Words have an awesome impact.
The impressions made by a
father's voice can set
an entire trend of life into motion.

Gordon MacDonald

Father was the dark-skinned, dark and woolly-haired giant who came and went between our little home and the outer world—our sure defender, last authority, and ideal of mighty power. One child's father may be a general or a president and another's a storekeeper or a tenant farmer, but the child's mind levels them: each of these men, so differently placed is to his own child the hero of ultimate reliability.

William Pickens

Lucky that man whose children
make his happiness in life
and not his grief,
the anguished disappointment
of his hopes.

Euripides

113

When my parents came up to visit me at school on a weekend, I would spot them way off and I would run as fast as I could and kiss them hello. Not many boys at the school kissed their fathers, I noticed, and so about my third year there, when my parents came up, I approached them slower, aware that I was being watched. I kissed my mother and then I turned to my father. He knew

exactly what was going on in my mind and he
waited for me to make the first move.
When he saw it was not to be a hug or a kiss as it
had always been before, when he saw it was
to be a handshake, he smiled and put out
his hand to meet mine.

Philip B. Kunhardt, Jr., My Father's House

Fatherhood, for me, has been less a job than an unstable and surprising combination of adventure, blindman's bluff, guerrilla warfare, and crossword puzzle.

Frederic F. Van de Water

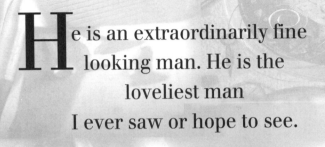

He is an extraordinarily fine looking man. He is the loveliest man I ever saw or hope to see.

Susy Clemens, age 13, about her father, Mark Twain

Romance fails us and so do friendships, but the relationship of parent and child, less noisy than all others, remains indelible and indestructible, the strongest relationship on the earth.

Theodor Reik

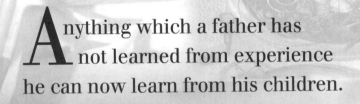

Anything which a father has not learned from experience he can now learn from his children.

Anonymous

What do I owe my father? Everything. He was my best friend: a parent who knew how to be patient with an unruly child; a preacher of joyful faith, who practiced what he taught; a good companion in the woods and the library; a fearless man with a kind heart. Every day I give thanks for him.

Henry Van Dyke

First and foremost, they are our fathers; and whatever magic we had with them, even if for just a few of our very early years, profoundly affects us for the rest of our lives.

Cyra McFadden

ACKNOWLEDGEMENTS

Barrett, Kenneth: Passage from "Promises" by Kenneth Barrett taken from *Fathers and Sons: An Anthology*, edited by David Seybold. Copyright © 1992 by Kenneth Barrett. Grove/Atlantic, Inc. Used by permission of the author.

Holmes, Reginald: "Letter To Dad" by Reginald Holmes taken from *Family Issue Ideals*. Vol. 24, No. 3. May 1967. Ideals Publishing Co. Our sincere thanks to the author who we were unable to locate.

Kunhardt, Philip B., Jr.: Passage taken from *My Father's House* by Philip B. Kunhardt, Jr. Copyright © 1970 by Random House Publishers.

Other Penbrooke Books You Will Enjoy:

Love Letters To Remember (ISBN # 1-889116-02-5)

Letters to Mother (ISBN # 1-889116-00-9)

Joy of Christmas (ISBN # 1-889116-06-8)

Sister of Mine (ISBN # 1-889116-08-4)

Everlasting Friendship (ISBN # 1-889116-04-1)

Significant Acts of Kindness (ISBN # 1-889116-01-7)

A Timeless Gift of Love (ISBN # 1-889116-05-X)

A Tribute to Mom (ISBN # 1-889116-12-2)

The Little Book of Happies (ISBN # 1-889116-03-3)

My False Teeth Fit Fine, But I Sure Miss My Mind (ISBN # 1-889116-07-6)

To order additional copies of this book, or any of our other books, call toll-free 1-888-493-2665